THE BLUE EYE OF EARTH

PITT POETRY SERIES

Nancy Krygowski and Jeffrey McDaniel, *Editors*

THE BLUE EYE OF EARTH

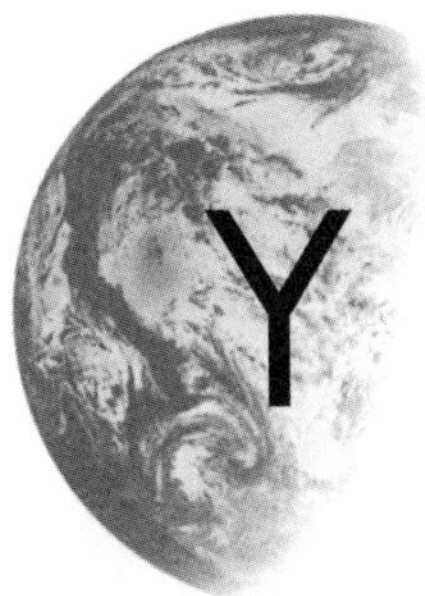

Beckian Fritz Goldberg

Poems

Published by the University of Pittsburgh Press, Pittsburgh, Pa., 15260

Manufactured in the United States of America
Printed on acid-free paper
10 9 8 7 6 5 4 3 2 1

ISBN 13: 978-0-8229-6838-2
ISBN 10: 0-8229-6838-X

Cover photograph: *Earthrise*, taken on December 24, 1968, by Apollo 8 astronaut William "Bill" Anders

Cover design and book design by Alex Wolfe

Publisher: University of Pittsburgh Press, 7500 Thomas Blvd., 4th floor, Pittsburgh, PA 15260, United States, www.upittpress.org

EU Authorized Representative: Easy Access System Europe, Mustamäe tee 50, 10621 Tallinn, Estonia, gpsr.requests@easproject.com

In Memoriam

MY MOTHER
Betty Fritz
1918–2025

MY BEAUTIFUL HUSBAND
Richard Goldberg
1936–2025

CONTENTS

Be happy

—ON GRAVESTONE FROM NECROPOLIS OF KAMIROS,
FIFTH CENTURY BC

THE BLUE EYE OF EARTH

1

MUSIC AT AN EXHUMATION

This spring they dug up Pablo Neruda to see if he was poisoned.
A guitar, a violin, played beside the grave overlooking the sea,
though what good is a grave that overlooks the sea. Still,
the desert blooms a thousand golds and yellows, summoning
every possible memory. Still, the moth like a dusty ghost
tries to unbutton the window at night. And I can tell you
on the same night in the east Antares burns like a rose that has seen hell.
It is the night of my fifty-ninth birthday, the resinous scent
from sweet acacias drifts the cool dark, and I am asking what happened.
What happened to the Bulgarian who gave me ten dollars once
when I was young and desperate for bus fare home. What happened
to Mrs. Biggs in the fourth grade who'd warn me before she read
the sad part of a story. What happened to the first boy who kissed me.
What happened to my father. It is a time of wonder—
Neruda has flown to Santiago. They have X-rayed his body
and studied the images. A wine jug hung from a tree. The sacra's
eaten face. What happened to Kathleen—the girl I discussed my first
kiss with, the girl I smoked my first dope with and the girl who called
years later when her marriage was unraveling but by then I was bound by
my own misery and could help no one. What happened to
my friend "South Carolina" who I met in jail. What happened to everyone?
All day the wind has blown and I'm tired of it. It blew
a dead bird onto my patio. A flicker. One day you're driving
home from work and it comes to you, you haven't seen that cashier
with the thick spectacles at the supermarket in a while. Maybe he

got fired. Maybe he got a better job than ringing up
canned goods all day long. Me? I'm just trying get a dead bird
up with a shovel and then I don't know where to carry him. Tonight,
the air is heavy with pollen. Everything swollen with resurrection.
The sad part of the story when I was nine was the part where
the dog died and since I already knew the story I told Mrs. Biggs
it was OK and braced myself. Still, I covered my ears until
she looked up and nodded. Still, I remember the name of the dog
was Jack, that they buried him in the prairie and later
moved away. Some things kill you every time. When you look up
it is spring again and some tough Camaro, woofers booming
from the trunk, vibrates in your breastbone with its stronger heartbeat.
There are no lights along the road until the city limits. I listen
as the throb goes soft with distance and the desert's flat quiet again.
It is late; nothing can happen now. No one ever dreams
they will be fifty-nine, that spring has come fifty-nine times
and fifty-nine blossoms in the acacia, sweet as laundered sheets,
tannic as tobacco, perfume the blind air where they have lost track.
It was just last week the Venezuelan government announced
plans to exhume Hugo Chávez to see if he'd been deliberately
infected with cancer. This same man who had them bring up
the bones of Simón Bolívar so he could converse with them.
Is the whole of South America crazy? Is it crazier than North America
where no one mentions death except those who don't believe in it,
the body a mere burden to be discarded, gently, in the brush of the arroyo

by someone with a shovel—is it crazier than heaven? What happened
to the crazy kid from the halfway house who kept sending me his paintings
because I'd been nice to him when I taught night school English.
They were a gibberish of color on cheap canvas board. Most of them
looked like they were on fire though sometimes there were pencil
figures with round heads and sometimes buildings with windows
behind the paint. I kept them in the closet mainly as evidence
for I was positive he was going to murder me. But after five years
the paintings stopped coming, and he has let me live at least
to fifty-nine which somehow seems as ancient to me as it did when
I was sixteen. Night still smells of creosote. The first stars smart
from the blue blackness. Say
the painter of those paintings came back and murdered me, don't come back
years later and raise me from the ground to prove it. There comes
a time when the body no longer desires to be seen, it is done being,
unrecognizable even to itself had it an eye left. It's purpose
was always beauty, not justice. All that is left of Neruda is bone.
Doctors extract some marrow and send it to North Carolina
for tests. I have died fifty-nine times
of spring. I have fifty-nine times rehearsed myself as ghost. I have been a figure
drawn in pencil behind the flames. What happened to me? What
happened to the night that drove past fields of blind sugar beets, past
the electric castle of the power station, into the desert, did it
ever stop? What happened to Edgar Poe? I once climbed over
the churchyard's iron fence to leave a bud on his grave, and also

a tube of lipstick, deep cerise, should he rise some evening and haunt
the misty docks of Baltimore with the need to feel desire, with
the need for a mouth. In truth, we die of nothing else. In truth
we die the moment we love. In truth, you kill me with your face.
Not so long ago, the Italians opened Petrarch's tomb to take his skull
and reconstruct his face but they found in it a man's body
and the shattered skull of a woman. Someone had stolen the left arm.
Perhaps his eyes were deep set and dark as spring night,
miro pensoso le crudeli stelle, che m'anno facto di sensibil terra—
I gaze pensively at cruel stars that have created me of sentient earth.
This night smelling of incense and iron, blind with thought. This *not.*
Neruda is not Neruda. The night drags its violet hair. Your face is not
your face. Think of the man who stole Petrarch's head, was he not
like us—raising an empty lantern as if what was once there
still flamed. It is spring. The orange moon arrives like a painting.
Why did you die? Why did you die and leave me shapeless
with fifty-nine holes, with fifty-nine letters in the alphabet. And Pablo Neruda
poisoned. Pablo, I knew that crazy kid was in love with me
and I could not stop it. I could not stop my body from appearing
in his mind. From lighting fifty-nine fires. *Miro pensoso le crudeli stelle . . .*
In his last painting I thought I saw a window far in the orange yellow,
the flames shaped like golden hysterical women, the soft green-hackled
sprites of space, and understood why he might pour gasoline
around an empty house one night and light a match, why when
the cops came he might still be standing outside with his gas can

watching form eat form. It was felony transcendence. That far gold window
extinguished in the back of the closet behind the sad-sleeved coat I never wore.
These nights, half-cool, I stand outside the house—as if I'm waiting
but for what I couldn't say. When they dug up Allende, two springs ago,
they examined the hole left by the AK47 he'd held under his chin
and confirmed the cause of death was suicide. All the arms in the earth,
all the teeth, hips, ears and knees in the earth, yield us nothing. The body
has told us all it knows which first and last is separation. Between
hunger, heat, habit, heavenly touch, helplessness, beauty and
more beauty, and more hurt—like music at an exhumation
it is the difference between a silence, and a violin, and then a silence.
Still, the desert blooms a thousand golds and yellows which are steeped in night
and exude memory. Still, the ashy moth falls open to the same page with
its mysterious watermark. And spring rises from the underworld alone
and dies of nothing.

BIRDS OF DARKNESS INHABIT THE NIGHT, STARS ON THEIR FOREHEADS

—Edmond Jabés

I pissed away the day, beautiful as it was. The moon came,
a quarter moon in the sheerness of evening when solid things
take on a delicate inkiness. Maybe your life is better. Maybe
it has consequences. Though I've called my mother
every night since he died. Honestly, some nights
I'm tired. I don't want to talk to anyone. Grief
is such work. At night I can't tell which star
goes with which when I look for constellations.
I didn't used to give a shit about constellations. I've grown sadder,
so now I look at everything a long time. There's a channel
on TV that you can tune in to any time to see a live satellite
picture of the earth from space. Here it's channel 287.
Sometimes it's mostly glare; but at 7:28 p.m., Tuesday
October 12th its white-maned azures hold, still as childhood,
above the dark Americas, and us. Is anyone else watching—
there are no car chases and no pretty girls, just a planet
in the place it belongs. Suffering is not important. Someday
standing here amazed you did not die at twenty-five, your genius
misunderstood, you'll say, So here we are old friend, and you'll mean
you. After that, a cigarette, or whatever your poison. See,
a yellow gondola has drifted ashore the shoulder
of the mountain like a quarter moon. Sometimes fancy
is true. Now you say you can see it, you say not exactly.
Night around you like a black perfume. Remember that?
Suffering is only what we call it. Nothing abates it and

nothing has no name and yet we are awake
and yet the flashing jacamars roam Mexico, the wing's green
luminescence & long stun of afternoon traffic that's going
nowhere but just wants to go. Here sing Goddamn, like
the man said. Tonight my mother tells me the dog has started
sleeping in the empty side of the bed. You could search your
whole life and never find an ending more simple
if you want to sleep tonight: I got up finally
and I pissed the day away, had lots of coffee, saw the bobcat
through the window, the one that's been hanging around,
nonchalant and brown and wondered why just his ears,
just the tail's tip, were marked with black and white.
When the universe took the time. I went from window
to window making sure I got a good look. Bought
some crap for dinner. After, I walked outside
and watched the slow stars rise from the airport
to the south. I saw they were bigger than the mind. Of what
this convinced me, I couldn't say. The sky like
the lowing iris in a flame, all that through and blue
and through. I mean the staring which is feeling.
You know. As sure as you are never here
no more. OK, I piss away most the night too
getting nowhere, sometimes just outside the door
where the world goes vast & the secretive
desert mice run out into the spotlight the light's

cast in the gravel near the steps. I will never have my life.
I will never hold it in my arms. Beautiful is that was—
the breast of Asia's shining up through the clouds at 2:15 a.m.
the satellite shot of its own foot thrust out in weightlessness
and we see from an inhuman distance down the dark
the lone insane living jewel—
and still ask why. Will someone tell us. Oh you,
you, you, my grief and lovelessness, little husband dog
stars, and you. The first pink light
stays low and lights the bushes black and fitting
back into their crooked forms. Here we live in hours, that's
all we know. I felt like doing nothing. And all day
the satellite gazed back through its tripod arms
as if we'd already left the earth behind. A few billion years
from now, they say, as our sun dies we'll have to. Or
have learned to harness the gravity of asteroids and move
the planet. Move sky bird empty bed and all. Anyone
who has reason to believe we'll still be here by then please
stick a knife through your sorry heart. And talk to me.

AN OCCUPATION

The world will end in pink. Those clouds just above the horizon
burn like lanterns. Overhead the dark monsoon clouds move in swiftly—

with their terrible eye sockets and long
gray beards they are the faces of the prophets.

Then the light dies. The wind is hoarse with ozone and the
continents move together. It is rare temper for the desert
where mostly it looks
                                        like the world has already ended

in an eternity flat and brown and the hot atomic white light of the afterlife. This
judgment is different: The air gets heavy, then sweet. Dust begins
to fly. Then the clouds dark as grapes . . .

Later in your life you'll study the sky each day like me
                                                                                an occupation

of the increasingly mortal. And small children
who see lambs and buffalos. Then forget. The birds have hidden,
east the sky is a mirror's back. All this drama of light and air
before the drops come fat as berries, a few at first, then the roof
is roaring. I think of someone I've lost

how vast he is—how oblivious
to all this furious touching. My body

is his relic. My mind is all he was. If the world has not taught us
tenderness, what have we done, what will we.
Even the coyotes
have retreated to their caves. Thunder whip-cracks, lightning
flashbacks the desert, the houses on the mountain, the air an amethyst
blink.

The rain wants to drive itself into everything. I want

everything. Today in the mail was a letter about the legal slaughter

of wolves in Montana and how I can stop it. That was depressing so I went
out to look at the sky,
thinking there was no room for innocence anymore.
Thinking that some day there'd be no wolves, the rhinoceros extinct,
the elephant a legend, none in the clouds,

that this may happen in my lifetime.

The air
was close as sweat. Toward dusk I saw the faint pink glow

at the end of things, my neighbor's great mesquite against it
somehow delicate, a black lace. I missed you
and missed you. Then the rain filled you like a mouth.

MY SCIENCE

We had our own Gila monster in second grade.
He was de-fanged so he couldn't hurt us, though we
were wary of his black flickering tongue. That year
we also learned the correct way to pick up
a scorpion without getting stung. The scorpions
we had had no venom. They were just teachers.
Our teacher was married to a scientist
and she had a Russian name. I don't know how old
she was but she seemed to me at the time as old
as the creased rock we studied on field trips
which bore a fossil print of palmetto right there
in the mountain behind the stadium at the university.
One day we went into a building nearby, up
to see her husband in a white lab coat among
the glass tanks of snakes longer than your daddy.
Our Gila monster had his own glass tank
that sat on the long shelf along one classroom wall
all through math and valentines with paste and
lunch and April Fools. Sometimes I'd study the writing
on his dull black body like pink-orange petroglyphs
we'd seen when we studied the Hohokam.
I had not lived in the desert long. We'd moved
from the Midwest the year before. If sometimes it seems
the whole year of second grade was sunlight and a stranger,
I know my science is inexact. I don't remember if

I knew that Gila monsters spend most of their lives buried
in dark burrows, or secreted in some rocky shelter.
How grateful ours must have been when school
was out and night fell. Life is odd. I don't remember
a single face from second grade, even the teacher's
is vague as geography. But I can see the windows around
the room, their blue sky and bleached brown grass
as if that little world were empty now, returned
to what it meant to be before us. This distant morning
I caught the cat in concentration crouching at the glass
sliding door as the lizard lumbered from the dirt.
When I saw the markings on that studded body,
the ancient text, I knew he was the monster
I stroked with one hand long ago when my hand was small,
his skin as dry as mother's beaded purse, as if I too had been
underground, asleep since then, and time passed, and only now
was in the world again watching the dry wizened head,
the blink, the body still a body, but newly strange.

PETALOUDES

On the island of Rhodes
we walked into a valley of butterflies.
The trunks of the trees
were ruffled with dark yellow wings.
The branches rippled with them.
The rocks bloomed with them.
It was the smell of the Oriental
sweet gums, of aromatic raisin, that called
the tiger moths floating
from light to shadow, delicate
mortals, landing on heaven
which grew here. The air
buzzed electric with cicadas
as if the heat were singing.
Summer is beautiful, the one
memory loves most. Thousands
like gold leaves refusing
to fall, fluttering under the breeze,
folded to sleep upright
on the trunks. Later that day
we looked down from a cliff
at the edge of the island
into the blue blown
glass of the sea. The view
has been the same

for centuries, water, sky,
hardly a horizon—
Standing there was like falling.
Standing there was already
long ago. We rode back
to town in the bed of someone's truck
with only one wheel centered
in the front as it bumped and
wheezed along the road. On
the way down the smell of pine pitch
from the aleppos hung in the heat
and sometimes we breathed in
the sweet stink of gasoline until
we arrived and the air again
was full of the sea. Summer
in no year. Summer of no sleep.
We lay nights in that room barely
bigger than the bed
beneath the one small window,
naked, too hot for the sheet, listening
to the town cats cry on the roof
above us. All night they were
agonies. All night they were desire.
Goddamn them. The tiger moths, too,
were nocturnal, swooning in the perfumed

trees to mate before the end of
the season. They had starved themselves
for this moment. Summer
of sweat and honey
fed to us a century later by
mysterious means. Summer of
flying flowers. At night the water
was black, the sky was black. Both
had a moon—
You could hardly
tell where the world was—
Your body, my body,
the valley trembling, and beauty
the birth of grief.

BEES ON COCAINE

We live in the wake of bullshit.
But what's left of the evening is pink
electrified along the naked line of the horizon
the desert's three trees darkening against it,
veil, cluster, shadowy pompadour. Some things
we understand. A clock speeding through
outer space will run slow. There are countries
that want to kill other countries. This is why any
field is sad. Net, taper, black lace. Nobody
says please anymore. Nobody minds.
The sun goes down like a fever. And sonofabitch
there's the moon. If there weren't, we'd
fly off the earth and take the oceans with us. Maybe
we will. Ironwood, mesquite.
Inkbleed. For two years Mother talked
to the ashes in the closet, Why did you leave me
in such a mess? A truck goes down the road,
hauling a boat, and the aftershush pulls away
until your mind comes back. Dark matter
rushes through us at every moment. O Cosmos, tonight
I am going to the grocery store where the sparrow
flies o'er the apples. The cashier says
the bird's been in the store for two months and
she doesn't know why they don't call someone.
Who do we call. Ice, cigarettes, coffee. All summer

Scorpio hangs around the house. The voice
from a passing car radio carries until the black
bushes along the arroyo sing *you been gone*
and one long subsiding vowel. What you hear is not
what you get. Not at all. We live in the wake
of the spill, the swindle, the big explosion. Abandon
Earth. The human being talks to himself in his head
at the rate of three hundred to a thousand words
a minute. The government funds a study of bees.
I pour the strong black coffee over ice, sit out on the step
with the voice. Speaker, listener, the wailing ephemera.
I wish, I wish, amen amen amen amen amen amen
amen amen. Mother says these days Stepfather
often can't remember where he is but they're OK.
We don't say soon he won't know her. Sometimes
she hears him argue in the living room with someone
who's not there. No other bird. But he's happy, she sings.
Hypothesis. Experiment. Constellation. In the study
they applied a drop of liquefied cocaine
to the back of each bee, then watched as the blow
sank into their nervous system and they rose
without knowing that they were bees, that they were
each a particular bee and that a bee was a cluster of
molecules as every living thing bewildered
by an ecstasy, sudden, magnifuckingfying bee

and being, as if joy were all along some higher
form of confusion. Oh, they did what bees did, they
walked into the flower. They danced if they found
food. But the bees on coke danced more
for less, even if the larkspur held only a taste.
Amen. The night sky is clear and I've been looking
for constellations. I have found Antares rowing
in place like the light of a boat. I sit with the house
and all my books and things in it strapped to my back
like a sack, cup in my hand as if I'm going somewhere
far in the black heat, the exhaust of August
while the sparrow in produce floats over
the wild apple forests of Kazakhstan and on
to a pyramid of canned corn. Here, the light of a plane
is crossing the shape of a teapot I've traced in the sky.
Closer, I hear the hum, I feel its slow arc pull
the top of my head. At night we are bodies who think
we are not bodies. At night we look up
into nothing and speak. Sometimes all we are
is a lonely conversation between the one who loves
and the one who dies which soon enough
will be the same, floating in the darkness, the brief
vibrations of an even briefer form, unlistened to,
unheld, unhelpable and eventually insane among
the quarks and muons more fit to be

than being is. Finally, Mother gave the ashes
to the sky in the eye of the lake. Why did you
leave me. Another car falls, & another
on the skirt of the last, drifting away where the road
shrinks to point and the landscape ends. All right,
I'm going in. Miserable listener,
I leave you the hostage sparrow who scats
on the shores of lettuce. We are the wake
of stars, our true deaths of long ago, and there are
planets that want to kill other planets, there are
messes left. Some things we know. Give freebase
to bees and you get stoned bees. This is why
every government is sad. No one gets off the phone
anymore. I hear what I hear. No wind.
Desert beetles tick against the lit window, fall
back into the fallen light on the ground. I'm not willing
to forget this. But we will forget this, switching
off the light for mercy and touching our way down
the dark hallway of the house to the breath
of someone we love and who has forgotten us
in their deep sleep. What can we do but undress
ourselves before them as always in their last
bloom for our last touch, our one drop left, and dance
more for less.

ENCHANTED EGG #1

At the far end is the bed in the meadow as you always dreamed. Nearer, on the couch there is a grandmother and beside the grandmother a small child, so small her feet barely reach past the outer edge of the cushion.

The grandmother is telling the girl the story of when they cut her stomach open and what a big white scar she had. Above, on the wall behind the couch, three small stained-glass windows with pieces milky green, glowing purple, transparent gold, let in the last sunlight. They cut her stomach open and then took most of it away. Those doctors, those doctors, what did they do with all the stomachs. Now, she tells the child, hers is the size of a walnut.

Meanwhile at the far end is the meadow with the bed in it, the curved blue sky, clouds like sugar roses. Space itself is little here at the end of summer, small as the porthole your eye fills where the delicate walls begin to swell. But things are distorted because of the view.

On the half-wall separating the living room from dining room hangs a full length oil portrait of a young man. Grandmother tells the little girl the young man was her brother. He was a soldier and died of mustard gas in the war. A horrible death. Your body blisters, your nose bleeds, you can't breathe. She sighs, He was seventeen . . .

Seventeen is very far away and old enough to die the girl supposes.

Beyond, the grasses and cornflower and wild buttercup surround the bed, the sumptuous linens, the silken white quilt, the gleam of cherry wood in the sunlight.

Now she can eat only a little bit at a time, Grandmother is saying, unlike that fat cow who lives upstairs.

ALIEN

Say you are there when the first one comes. Say one August night
you've left the door open because it's too hot inside. Bugs fly in and bang
the light bulb yellow white as the half-moon while you hold
the sheet with your arms spread, its smell a field somewhere else, fold.
Then you are not alone: Say it is more like a tree, silver in the dark,
and slender branches where leaves whisper. But it is not like
the trees here which are few, palo verde, mesquite,
and which have claws. Where are its eyes?
You are standing outside the door studying the living night.
Does it desire us, does
it, by its nature, merely extinguish—can that moth ping his one
bright planet until he burns? Say the tree is more like a recollection waiting
for its purpose, its shore white pebbles blank as eggs,
the lake quiet, the adults up late playing cards.
When you glance back at the light then turn and blink,
aura, aura. What is its intelligence? Its flower has no scent. Is more
its weightlessness its velvet rooms. It is useless to ask who's there—
Say it is the coat that appears in the closet, unfamiliar, the sleeves
too long to be yours, the key in its pocket to nothing you know.
And the faint ghost of sweet tobacco & somewhere else. More, more
like the horse and the row of red teapots that slide away
the moment you wake. There is no way to prepare for this.
Either love is coming
to stamp you out or it's not. Night hangs in the doorway humid,
and possible. Something—a rabbit—rustles in the brush. Say

it is also like the shush of cars dissolving in the distance, like
the name you can't remember, like the cry you can't get out. You
cannot touch its feeling. Where is its heart? Outside the trill
of toads from the arroyo lasts forever. You can feel its body.
It has no breath. Root in the dark seeking your water
with eight thin straggling arms, coming to touch you with
its hairs, trick you into blossom, kill you with memory, take you
somewhere and slap some logic into you. Is that terribly
inhuman? The swollen air aches for rain. The heat is fat with it.
Say it comes like a lion it comes
like a dove comes like storms of little jewels, the glitter-eyed
minerals of the earth, like nibbling, like licking, like sensational
weeping. The sweat shines on your breastbone beneath
the bulb light with its string hanging from the ceiling,
the shirts in a stack on the dryer. Come in, come in, my
death-flower, my yesterday, my double, little wave, my
first time and last time, silver branches breaching the mother dark.

CENSUS

We nurse the loons
who are failing, feathers tinged
blue-white from the mercury vapors.
The lake ruffles the moon tonight
and others see it, too–the soldier's
mother at home and not asleep,
the boys making camp near shore.
We've lived in the woods for hours,
long enough to know the eggs are sterile.
Summer's black as if fallen into a wound
from which a bird's falsetto throws itself.
Others hear it too, from dream, the runaway
camped with the dealer who gave her a ride,
and with his weird girlfriend Phil. It is not
a whole silence when it comes back—already
the milk to shape begins, long dawn,
the sedge. We walk the shallows in our boots.
We have come to warm the nests.
To offer transfusions. Clean the wings.
Though, black necklace by black necklace,
they disappear much as the gods have,
becoming merely names. Until not even
the names are attached to anything.

ENCHANTED EGG #2

When you look inside through the tiny porthole the lake looks back without blinking. A little girl has fallen from the raft floating away like a blue rooftop. She stands under water in clouds of silt and glitter. In the distance the undulant bed recedes till it is only horizon, the murky green light, the giant shape of father sleeping on the couch.

Great translucent rooms wander through one another. Even as her throat begins to burn, even as she is squeezed by a weight she can't see, brained-shaped shadows cruise the floor. Things are distorted; when she looks down at her foot it has magnified to the size of a pale blue potato stuck in the silky earth.

This is the world the day she doesn't die. Though it would be so simple. She's formed no ties, she can't read a clock. She might easily return to the oblivion she came from not so long ago.

At the end of the lake cupped on the white shore fathers and mothers are grilling meat. The sky is a dome as you always suspected.

It is a wonder that a lake can exist in so delicate a shell. The blue rooftop is skirting the shore. Below, the giant father rolls over on the couch, a fish flits by like a face, the water is absinthe, cat's iris, the lucid world, the breathless, even as a pair of legs comes toward her, it is solitaire, even as an aunt's arm reaches down, it is the moment she wants to look more than she wants to live and is cruelly rescued.

MY NEIGHBOR'S BODY

—for H. C. and for J. M. B.

What can I do tonight about the wild camels in Australia
whose herds the government will thin by aerial gunning?
The truth is all I do these days is watch the neighbor's hedge
of brooding oleanders sway, heavy with dark red blossom.
They are twelve feet high on his side of the arroyo
and hide his house. I don't know who lives there
but I know he has a truck and listens to the country station.
I can't help what I know and what I don't know
helps me. I stand out on the patio and smoke when I have work to do.
The blooms light their deep pink auras. All spring
my neighbor rattles things behind his house, throws
things on top of other things. It echoes. I haven't done
a good day's work since that day in school when I required
every poem henceforth to have in it a jacamar & hereby
have followed policy. It's the least I can do. My neighbor's song tonight
rues some faithless woman as he kills the engine, leaves
the radio on until the song is done. I have never seen his body.
I have never seen his faithless wife. I am on the side of
the black oleanders moving their great mind
under the little moon. They are fifteen feet high
and hide my house. It's been good, our not knowing each other.
He won't mind me still out on the patio not telling him
in Egypt once I heard camels call to one another
as they milled about and one by one kneeled for tourists to mount.

It is an ugly cry trapped, I can only say, like
the body of the letter *m* set on fire in their throats. In Cairo's heat
I moved around like royalty with a retinue of children
asking for American dollars. Like royalty I gave sometimes
and sometimes not. The hotel that summer was filled
with engineers working on the underground, work that stalled
each time they hit a buried wall or well of ancient kingdom,
and late afternoons they'd drink with Madam Ariana, the manager,
a Coptic Christian and a true believer
that ketchup was the cause of cancer and that opera
refined the soul. Tonight the moon holds its high white note over
the desert slopes. Here we are. What can we do
about camels in Australia stunned in the warm sheen of
their own blood? Dry yellow petals scatter on the patio.
They do this when they are alone. The world is full of the helpless,
seeing its one hand, the petals mounded briefly at the patio wall.
They whisper like the guard pulling us aside in the museum
where they kept animal mummies, mostly ibises and cats.
Their necks were wrung in sacrifice, their bodies emptied, filled again,
sewn and wrapped like dolls for gods who looked just like them.
For a dollar, he said, we could touch one. I know
everyone has to make a living. I don't know how my neighbor
does. He has somewhere to go to and somewhere to come back
and isn't that enough? Each day if I say he's happy he is happy.

If I say he is miserable he is. If I say put on a song sometimes
he does. Then I don't get much work done, another iridescent
jacamar lies unwritten. Tonight a hundred living things
chirr in the arroyo, the rest is quiet. Our lives are quiet.
We know what we know. I know my neighbor's body must have fire
like mine. It must have dim soft places no one's touched
for the longest time. I know it must rise sometimes at night
for no reason and then must go somewhere and sit. I don't know
what it is that aches. The body does not know how to speak
for itself. It stands out on the patio in the dark thinking this time
of John-Michael who has tattooed across his chest a line
from a poem he loves. He is brave. Think of the women
who'll face it there, a love no thing or woman will come between
and turn, and some come anyway. They'll know and not know.
There is no language there. The hedge shifts its thick
ocean of leaves in the wind and John-Michael is gone. Light
winks through. My neighbor is home, and if he knew he was
on my mind tonight he'd call the police. For all I know he's a cowboy
and would kick me to crap. For all I know he is
the police. For all I know he is lonely and would weep.
Beware of the neighbor. Beware the one who imagines you
in some form other than your own, filled with other desire, empty
of other emptiness. Beware the one who does not.
You are the gentle camel. You are the rufous-tailed jacamar.

Your blossoms hang open in the dark, riding the black
wave of oleander. And I am kissing my neighbor's full mouth, tracing
the moon above his left nipple. I am lying against his body,
reaching down and cupping them, gently, in my hand, for didn't we
come helpless into the world, my love, but we came anyway.

2

HENRY'S SONG

—for Nancy and Bill

Sometimes sitting in a friend's backyard on a fall evening
a thing comes to you. But then you second guess yourself.
You second guess yourself, and your grace is gone.
The cat dish is there by the step, overturned in the dry leaves,
the trees here taller than any trees in your dreams. You're afraid
if you stay here they might talk. And these nights
you only want to hear someone say, *Yes,*
I think of these things too . . . Nine o'clock, cold,
I couldn't see the stars for the trees, only the yellow light
of the back window doubled over on the ground. In it,
leaves laid with the kitchen. Then a figure passed:
My friend reaching up into the cupboard and looking lost
a little while. His wife bringing in a cup and dish. Both of them
standing by the sink talking maybe about buying apples tomorrow
or what movie or the jacket no one can find. Her hair
was still damp from the shower and haloed in the kitchen light
as he crossed into the next room blue with the blink of the TV.
That afternoon my friend had thought his cat was lost and we
searched for an hour but the cat had sunk into a deep pile of leaves,
lay half-covered and asleep. The cat who was not lost was named
Henry and he was dead a few weeks later of old age. At night
he'd come into the room where I slept and sit
staring down at the heating vent and, hours later, if I rose to pee,
he'd still be there as if waiting for something specific to rise
through the floor. But life inside the house that night was golden,

though then the kitchen was lonely, the cereal boxes misaligned
on the shelf, a nest of white bowls, mugs upside down in a row.
I thought someone will be left to open the cupboards after
we are dead and there see everything has stayed the way
we left it. Say yes, you think of these things, too. And that's
when the thing that came to me came to me and when I
second guessed myself I lost what the thing was. Sometime
it might return, but for now I'll say it was nothing. It was nothing.
Inside the house someone was asking, *Did you take Amlodipine*
and suffer heart failure? Do you live alone? Are you tired of carpet stains?
Do you need a loan fast? Yes. And yes and yes and yes.
I've thought of these things, too—standing at the window while skeletons
on TV marched toward a cartoon cowboy. It was even stranger
in the silence of early November, away from home. But life was gorgeous
in the house. The glazed red sugar bowl gleamed. Months
later, my friend told me sometimes he'd still mistake
the shadow, the wool scarf bunched on the chair, and think
it's Henry. As if the mind believed absence is a trick. For it can still see
everything. But the world asks, *Do you have crow's feet?*
Do you have enough to cover your funeral costs? Ever feel irregular?
Do you have trouble sleeping? That night the wind blowing
dead leaves sounded like a distant ocean, my fingertips
numbed with cold and the lit window held everything sacred
in its church. I saw that light the next day slanting as we walked
through an apple orchard and stopped at the mill for cider.

Farther on, we came to a large pond where pike and recluse sturgeon
lurked beneath the surface. On the bridge was a machine you'd put
a quarter in for a handful of food for the fish. I watched my friend
toss some in the water and the pond became alive with thrashing
bodies, the surface almost writhing with their gleams, the sound
of water laughing all around, and then they disappeared again,
the water like a shadow, deep, blue-green. And quiet. There was
a small breeze, an open field, a white clapboard building
on one side. Things are simple, that's what we forget.
When I slept that night I left the door ajar for Henry
who would come upstairs late for his vigil, the warm air
floating above the vent from some underworld
benevolent beyond his dreams. And when I woke later in the dark
as sometimes you do in a strange bed away from home
in a strange town with a moon and trees, I could feel he was there
long before I could distinguish his shape, before I could remember
exactly where I was. It came to me this loneliness is something we take
with us anywhere and not that we aren't loved, but that we aren't
loved forever. Life demands much less. The fish is purely
fish and that's enough. An apple wholly apple. Maybe it's enough
to be human, leave the door open, wait for a soul—which, if it comes, comes
like the half of the conversation we imagined because we
can't imagine that speaking is only speaking, even to the night,
the way we can't believe death is only death, the way we can't
stand outside a window on a fall evening in a pile of leaves in Kalamazoo

and not count ourselves among the missing. *Are you single and looking*
for your soul mate? Are you drowning in credit card debt?
Do you want more hair? Do you have trouble sleeping? Yes,
I have trouble sleeping. But, when it was my turn, I cupped my hand
and the machine filled it with food for the fish I scattered
over the water and they came like the rush of fat rain up
from the deep, glittering, swarming over nothing. It made me happy.
Then the green silence closing over them again. The little cat
waiting faithfully in the dark for his death and not complaining.
And us, knowing it is already a world without us, already a pond,
a cat, an orchard stuck with swords of light—
but the heart needs no reason for the belovéd.

ASSIGNMENT: EARTH

When Captain Kirk came back to Earth,
the oldest man to return from space, he
stepped out of the capsule and felt the full
weight of himself, William Shatner, on the Texas dirt.
The earth again was flat. The daylight
made him blink twice, as when one walks out from
a movie theater after a matinee. On his journey
he'd passed in an instant through the small breath
around the earth. Beyond, he'd seen Death—
stared into the empty black eye socket of space
and felt his molecules rearrange. A change

Kirk felt beaming down from the Enterprise
to Earth 1968. He and Spock dressed for
the occasion, Spock wearing a cap pulled down
over his Vulcan ears. A visitor from a secret
planet had beamed aboard the Enterprise
holding a black cat in his arms. He was on his way
to stop a nuclear war from destroying the earth.
Spock said there was no way to make a logical decision
whether to believe him. And so, when he left,
they followed. In another 1968 astronauts

left Earth to be the first to orbit the moon,
first to see its hidden face, the far side's cratered
surface. Tonight, the newly-landed Shatner
sees the same moon I do, a waxing crescent
almost white with light. I made it a rule
long ago, to go out each night no matter what
and look at the moon. No matter what—
even though tonight there's war, the same
bright sickle above Ukraine where
Russian soldiers have stormed the nuclear plant.
It's okay to be frightened, even if you are
a man from the future trying to save the planet
and I a woman of the present

looking at the moon through a black cat's eyes.
Time is running out. At the launch site
for the nuclear missile, Kirk and Spock watched
this man on a mission, Gary Seven, climb the gantry
along with his cat. But the clueless secretary
left alone in his earthly office accidentally
beamed him back. Time was running out.
The missile launched, Seven went to the computer
and put the exceivers on manual. Kirk and Spock
beamed down to stop him, still unsure
they could trust him. It was down

to seconds and Spock at the controls was having
no luck. Kirk had to trust his human intuition
and let Seven detonate the warhead above the earth
just in the time it took for his cat
to curl up on the couch. On his own couch

after his flight, Shatner had just finished an egg sandwich
still sore and stiff from the G-force of lift-off. Space
was black and vast, no twinkling stars, nothing
but death. The earth, a fragile, lone, oasis. Here
he would stay and pet his dogs, look out the window
at the lights of the San Fernando Valley,
the loyal moon, the past: Still the crew of Apollo 8
photographing Mare Tranquilitatis in '68
came out from behind the moon and began
to cross the front when they glanced through the window,
and saw, rising over the barren lunar horizon,
the blue eye of Earth. Sometimes looking back
is the whole point of the journey.

Tonight, at home it's another night of war, the Russians
hold workers at Chernobyl hostage shift
after shift while generators keep it going. Time
is running out. Tonight, the moon—no matter
what. A chill in the air, early spring. That night

after Kirk and Spock had left, perhaps
Gary Seven, his black cat purring in his lap,
leaned back in a comfortable armchair and
closed his eyes as the mini-skirted secretary
served him a gimlet. After all, he'd just
saved the world. Tomorrow he'd beam
back to his planet. *Astral Weeks* on the stereo,
he sipped his drink, melting into the music. It was
his last night on earth, and who
hasn't imagined what they would do then?

MY RAIN

I miss the rain we had days ago
I want it to come back, I want it to
bring the smells it used to bring
when I lived in the desert. But it is not
that rain and it smells like the little streets
and winter lawns and the secret cafés
that lurk in closed cars. Give me
a cigarette. No, don't. The day is clear,
cold as the floor, cold as doorknobs, and
memory is walking in and out of every room
not sure what it's looking for, not sure
who's there. The apple tree in the yard has
lost all its leaves. Who knows if it will
bloom again come warm weather?
Who knows how to grow old? Tonight
the year ends. Late I hear the *sh shhh* of
the ocean, coming, going, coming,
going, an ancient sound known by all men
like a lover's sleep. The cats patrol the house,
sniffing for ghosts. Midnight the neighborhood
pops with firecrackers for at least
ten minutes, falls back into a hush
where you can imagine staying here,
out of sight in some corner, hidden from
death so it passes you over. No one

would ever know unless you came out of
the house. Then the rain would bring
any smell you wanted, the resiny
sweetness of the desert, the savor of
gasoline, the smell of the sheets
after lovemaking . . . as long as you didn't
give yourself away. But even this
couldn't stop the longing that grows
every day of your life till your arms
reach out from your stomach
and your lips spill from your ears
into the sea. Be kind to the night with
the new year on its breath and carrying
the dreams of everyone where we
are naked, or lost, or pursued by
murderous men. For rain, that old
business, will raise the present from the earth
like incense and tonight the neighbor's
Christmas lights glow into my room,
red, green, gold, red, blue, jeweling my sleep.

CONCERNING THE TERRESTRIAL

Once the town did not touch you here. There was nothing:
beet field, lettuce, sky where now this window looks across
to a window in the wing opposite. If I stand I can see
the finest bones of a poplar rooted two stories below. It's December
in Mesa, Arizona, and I cursed you on the way here for
staying in the town I'd left at eighteen though it had changed
and I got lost as all I recognized were signs of where I'd been.
The mortuary, Milano's music store turned thrift shop, and that
corner, that neighborhood of orange trees, until I sailed
through a red light near the hospital I didn't remember and luckily
only one car honked and everyone lived. Mid-afternoon, the hotel's near
deserted and the drift of our smoke through the screen goes
unnoticed though I like the thought cloud of white kush spreading, falling
out over the town that used to send schoolgirls home if
their bra straps were discernible beneath their white
blouses. I like it the same way I liked a heavenly stratus
of Marlboro Reds rising up the wall we leaned our backs against
beneath the narrow windows where Brother Nelson droned.
We should have been in 5th hour Biology. Though truant there,
across the street behind the building belonging to the Latter Day
Saints, we were learning something about the levels of the terrestrial,
telestial, and celestial, as Brother Nelson explained we must all
become gods. Eventually. We'd shake our heads and
Craig would mutter something wise and wry. We'd baptize
their ancestors with smoke. For now, in room 206, only

the poplar, the spaces marked off below on the asphalt, are wise
to us. The sun, late gold and warm. Tick tock. We talk about who had
the craziest schizo student, our aging parents, how once in Chicago
I saw a man drag his fiancée on her knees down the carpeted
hotel corridor, cursing her hung by one arm in his grip,
and we both forget why I began telling you. Silent. For a while
I've been trying to figure out the one car parked, a license plate
inscrutable from here. Then a man comes out the orange door
first floor in the wing across and swings a chair out to face
the pavement, props the door open, goes back inside. You
want to know what the symbol is on his license plate, figuring
as I do, the parked car there is his—the man now sitting by his door,
plastic hotel-issue wastebasket turned over to serve
as his cocktail table, the plastic cup full. He reads the paper,
stretching his bare feet in front of the topsiders
capsized on the strip of grass. By the time you get up
and turn on the fan to blow the air around and decide to
make some coffee and unwrap the cups saying you'd been
listening again to *The White Album*, the man we know as
the only other man alive in this hotel is smoking his cigarette
and I say clearly he doesn't know where he is. You can legally
take a gun into a bar in this town but you can't fire up
smoke. This town where my girlfriend and I got
kicked out of the movies for clapping and whistling during
Bonnie and Clyde. We were fourteen and thumbed

a ride home with some guys who ended up making us
hold their dicks. We wouldn't have said then that we were
lucky, but oh, we were lucky. We terrestrials. Even now the coffee
here is pretty good for what it is, a shot to get us on our feet,
down the stairs, around the building and through the parking lot,
casually, for a closer look at the license plate so unreasonably
in question. The sky is clear blue, sun strong like every day,
and the flower or the hatchet or the bird we imagined on the plate
turns out to be the flag of South Carolina which is a palmetto
and a crescent moon and I think the prettiest flag in America,
no shit. I would lie down in it. You're busy trying to find
the stairs again. But let us sit down. At least. We've got
the time and sit on an island of grass near the Out Of Order
swimming pool. It's winter grass, planted for the season, a green
so new it hurts. Green as my South Carolina palmetto. More and more
when I am somewhere I am somewhere else, recurring
exponentially as I get older. It is the great disease and I
am dying of it, nothing more than a host. Up in the room
I listen to you talk to your father on the phone. He won't agree
to meet for breakfast until he knows the exact street address
of the pancake house. The cocktail man takes his chair inside,
calling it a day. Years from now there won't be much
of this day we recollect, and so many days I suppose, in the end,
we can't account for. We know we spent some years going to school.
We know we lived on a farm till we were six. But all we said

or wanted to, all we did, all the times we woke up and stood
before the sink are lost except perhaps for the time we broke our arm
or the day the dog died, or the thing that someone said that hurt.
So it's no wonder I got lost driving through the town I came from
which, by now, is mostly a blank, like high school, like half of
all the year's one's married. Then, like that, I passed a street whose name
suddenly bloomed the boredom of being seventeen and
waiting to be gone. *What tripe, what bullshit, what wasted years . . .*
Craig had written in the yearbook I kept a week then tossed.
And he was right. So much is unremarkable and daily, it's a wonder
life gets lived. How did you spend your life, God asks. You say,
Well, I went to school, I ate dinner most every night, got a job,
must have gone to the post office at least a hundred times, raised
a family, visited a few places, watched 9/11 on TV—until you feel like
one long etcetera. Exhale. In the flicker, we are in the Supernal
Mystery of Existence, I'm telling you where the hotel is in the eons
there used to be citrus orchards, places to make out. You're filling me in
on a friend who's being sued while you walk me out to my car
past the grass and the chained gate to the pool. But these are the moments,
these nothings, these betweens. Whoosh of freeway noise, the sun
reflecting hard. You turn the wrong way, we're near the lobby, so you
walk through. I follow. If our lives are spent doing
nothing in particular, nothing important, at the Something Rancho Inn,
if countless Thursdays in December pass and leave no candle, if
innumerable appointments make no names for themselves, or us,

staring out the window, lying on the couch and lain upon by smoke,
let us meet there again. Let us sit down. The grass is almost
lit from within. Let's lie back and wait for
your wife to return, wait to see what I pick up for dinner on the way home,
wait for your father to show up at the pancake house, bide
our time as if it's not all about dying here within sight of a town
I knew once or thought I knew, at least, in some earthly sense, oh,
Brother Someone—the last time I saw Craig before he put a gun in his mouth
I was eighteen. We had a pleasant exchange at the mall not far from here.
Nothing. Tick tock. Just before dusk the traffic on the overpass
is a white haze of glare and dust and, above, a streak of gold, scud
of dark blue. So much is unremarkable. In the parking lot we hug, say hey
it was good. Tonight, you're going with the in-laws to see the Christmas lights
around the Mormon temple. I'm remembering on the drive home
summer evenings a tribe of us, none whose name or face I can recall
would bike to it, the large lawns with spotlit looming cypresses.
At seven or so the sprinklers would come on and we'd run through,
cooling off, then take our bikes across the street to the Dairy Queen.
I'd order a lime slush. But I'm not stopping anywhere tonight. I like
the drive, lit windows like honeycombs in the darkness,
the snuff black expanses of desert between. I like it the way I like
not being somewhere: Anonymous and Unlocatable—like the soul,
Brother Nelson, the holy ghost turning its little trash bin over,
setting its cocktail atop, leaning back in its chair outside some door,
letting the day fall while giggling strangers walk through the parking lot

twice. Wasted. Wasted. Tonight, I'm thinking Mexican take-out, you're
staring at wire camels wrapped in white lights headed atwinkle for
Bethlehem across the wide temple lawn. This is it. Incongruous reindeer
peep out from the shrubbery. I'm admiring the billboard unicorn
pointing to the exit for a Gentleman's Club. So much is
unremarkable my friend. The stars come out every night. And regardless,
regardless of the man in Chicago twisting that woman's arm till she
cried out. Who, when he saw the crack of my door, hissed
down at her, *Bitch, now look what you've done*. She was limp
staring into nowhere like an animal playing dead. It's too simple
to say she should just wake up and leave him. He's got her. He's got
all of us who come back to suffering. For love. Look at her,
yanked up from her knees and stumbling. Is she stupid? Or does she know
not loving him would make the blows less bearable, the body
pointless, the heart moot. I'd said, Stop. Not that I was brave so much
as pissed some fuck was making noise outside my room at 1 a.m.
My fear was that night I made it worse
simply by being witness, that he'd really take it out on her
once they were alone. The city lights behind, it's almost quiet now,
the road into the foothills, houses flickering blue TVs.
Blesséd is the man whose day is melting slowly into the matter of
a touchdown, blesséd the woman slipping into her romance, the boy
tranced by cyber-swordsmen decapitating evil androids
spouting buckets of alien blood. It's all we want. For time
to pass without taunting us. To let us sit a while without the burden

of heaven or where we go god forbid not to that town where I once
practically begged a boy to lie with me on a blanket in the orange grove
because even then I felt him slipping away from me into a life
I could not imagine and I did not think he'd love me
any other way. More than once I've missed the turn
toward home like this, by minding somewhere else and on a road
unlit by anything at night except sometimes a moon. Ahead
the houses of the mountain glow and I go slow because of cops
along this stretch who love to lie in wait. Tick tock. Though if I were stopped
tonight, I might mistake myself for the darker in a pair of fourteen-year-old girls
riding in the back of someone's souped-up Falcon holding each
some strange boy's electrified dick. From downtown through
the neighborhoods I felt it humming in my hand like the terrified
body of a bird I'd once tried to rescue which only made desire more
the mystery, and if, Officer, you find that plain unnatural, arrest me
cruising these last miles past dinnertime again, and appearing slightly
out of place. It's my tumor, my plague, my fever, my existential
carcinoma metastasizing everywhere like thought that blots out
thought that blots out thought until all you know is the one
you can't console is the one you were a day ago, a year. Then,
we didn't even have the sense to be afraid. They dropped us at the curb,
we stepped onto the lawn and it was springtime, we rolled our eyes
and grinned at one another and were fine. There, I say,
let us lie down. In the dark tonight beside the one we love
when we try to make it all make sense before we sleep, we'll end up

lost in South Carolina. Drift there through all the things we wanted or had
or didn't though what it all comes down to is a single stubborn
longing to stay right where we are and not be moved.
It is all here: Your crescent moon, your shoreline palmetto in the white mist.
Even if a man is beating his lover, even if a kid we knew is pointing
the gun down his throat and the boys are driving the girls out into the desert.
Your ice. Your chair. Even if that lost boy is turning from you
as you kiss him, even if the celestial pool is closed. Your grass.
Your flag. Your At Last. Let's buy the hotel. Let us stay here, again. Brother—
let each of us in this American romance with oblivion claim
our unremarkable place.

INDIGO

When I think of all the sick fucks in the world
I get sick: the man lighting into his boat, the woman
whipping the lilies. And the rabbit, rabbit
is a screamer. At home mother is splitting coffee beans
into two piles—*no good* and *no good bastards.*
I think everyone beautiful is on TV and someone
is smothering lingerie quietly and leaving
despite our cries. Whisper something good.
Even if just the curtains. But not *I love you.*
The boys are meeting at the lopped-off river
their nipples set like stun-guns
and all the idylls of spring shall fall, do
fall. They do not consider the thralldom of larkspurs
suffering, they do not, when the TV is on
think everyone is beautiful. Even the police.
The fat one snuffing the siren. The wife
sweating the berries. I was once
a small thing, breathing in childhood's indigo light.
You were once a small thing, breathing in
childhood's indigo, my indigo
my light. Of all the eaten
beaten twisted fucks who walk the earth,
I rock, I rock & then I listen. Someone
inked in the backyard twilight
recalls a night the sheets were ice & mother

took a hot iron to the bed. Whisper
something now. Even if just the TV.
We have our picture. We each have our picture.
The moth throwing itself at the porch light,
the man tied up in room nine. The man
punching the clock. And bees choke
buttercups along the highway, a trucker
kicks the tires, the diner spanks
the ketchup bottle over his fries. They
do not regard the jeremiad of the crickets, not
the bushes with their small red trumpets
hung like meat. The girls are wading into the woods
holding their razor blades
like matches. They will cut crimson
smiles in their skin, buzzing in the white
noise of the body. Whisper it now. The trumpeter
gagging the trumpet, the singer murdering his song,
the boy tearing legs
from spiders, and the pictures of missing girls
on TV are beautiful as their light forever
left twitching on the blameless walls.

HOT PINK

These are hard states. Jewels in
the opium. Haven't shit for days
I think, but Time's loose. Around here,
everything's loose, the trees are loose,
the roads, even Ned Horne that
ass from sixth grade has drifted
in and out my brain where memory is
mostly useless. Late spring with
the door wide open, nothing but
dark out, the purr of toads in the arroyo
like the endless trill of a pea whistle
drowning out the pitiful
glass-clinks of the crickets. Moths
fly to my lamps and waste their lives.
I cannot believe your absence
the way I believed your smell.
Tiny moths land in my cold coffee,
spread wings covered with the finest
lunar dust, stuck to the surface
while they nervously drown
unless I lift them out using
the pen I bought with a plastic
purple-hatted witch at top whose
arms pop up when you click
the button. Sometimes you can't

help love stupid. A cool breeze
walks around my room
messing with things then leaves
without saying *Aha!* These
are all conditions. Rubies
follow the cars. Loss is terrible
because of its precision. Me,
I never know if it's Wednesday.
I never know who I'll resurrect
from some obscure schoolroom at
the unlikeliest moment. The mind
snatches at everything. Tonight's
a full moon the color of candlelight
giant over the horizon
rimmed in hot pink. I stare until
I see it wobble. I can't help
marvel at its faithfulness
without which we are extinguished
without which the coyotes would not
let out their shrill cackles
like triumphant witches riding
their plastic brooms. My rescue moth
shivers in a wet stupor beside
the white cup stiff and stern as
a nurse. Nurse, how long,

I ask. I close my eyes. My palm
remembers your belly. These
are inadmissible circumstances—minus
minus minus this. I drink too
much coffee, I eat too much sugar.
Nothing is as easy as remembering.
The sorrow only lasts as long as the love.

THE DOOR

Even if tonight a man I like were to pull me close enough
to taste and with his breath suggest where we go next,
I wouldn't go. The last light glows pink in one long cloud
and soon the desert will be all black needles, and you'd think
at my age I'd be happy to be wanted by a man with a rough
beard and deep green eyes, to feel his hand slowly shape
my shape like evening. Once I rode all day in a bus just to meet
for a few hours a certain fisherman in a town near the bay. He
was married and I didn't care. What I remember most is the café
where he bought me a pretty dessert, something honeyed with a bright
half cherry on a pillow of whipped cream, thin almonds
scattered on the white plate. What else happened that brief evening
is gone though I imagine we did what lovers do and, parting,
arranged to meet again, for I recall us lasting nearly a year before
we simply drifted into other lives. I sometimes think if we knew
our days of longing, nights of skin and salt, eventually leave
nothing but a random detail, the dessert soaked with honey,
or the lettering on the side of a truck, we might not bother
trembling, we might not forget to breathe when someone's hand
just lightly grazes ours. But that's not why I wouldn't go. I'm all
for kisses. I'm all for grinding away in a squeaky bed in some
roadside motel. I'm for the rain coming down and a vine
climbing a trellis outside the door of each room where they
have not been together long, the lovers, not long enough to reach
the place where each one hurts so much they can no longer

find each other and it feels it will be like this forever.
Sometimes my husband wants to know why things can't be
the way they were in the beginning. He wants it to be like it was.
I am sad for him like an angel, the evening gone soft, the air
warm as skin. Why not look for the moon—
that way when the night's gone I might remember,
oh that was the night the May moon was almost full and gold,
and forget the rest as the mountain bleeds into blackness. Or I might
remember it was the night I realized the mechanic from the auto shop
left his cap in my car. On the cap it says *Cardinals* above the profile
of an angry red bird. I do not need this in my life.
Though my life might have been different if I'd fallen
for a mechanic, gotten lost in his strong arms, dizzy
pressed against his barrel chest, its nest of hair, and we'd
gone dancing at some country-western bar, and he'd begun
to call me *Baby.* That was the night, I'd tell my son someday,
when you were conceived. *Jeeesus, Mom*, he'd say. Or
I'll remember it was the night I couldn't find the moon. That night
at the café I was happy I was not in love with the fisherman.
Much of that year was miserable, but not because of him. I'd fallen
for a man who fell for someone else. Even after she was with him
I'd walk up to his door at night, press my ear against it. Listen.
I don't forget the young are desperate. Here it's still,
the desert toads are singing from the arroyo. They trill the same
long note for hours. Even after she was with him I could not forget.

The same long note. Though now I have forgotten everything
I saw in him that made me believe I had to have him. I didn't know then
that the desire to love is fiercer than the love itself. We see
the Beloved because we must. Yet in that space of time after
I gave up on him and while I was with the fisherman in whom
I saw only a fisherman, I was thankful. He bought me a dessert
I pretended to like, though the sugar made me shiver. I had seen in his face
he hoped it would please me and it had been so long since
anyone had hoped, I swallowed every bite. It was raining,
the café windows running, light above the table a bit too bright. He
would not remember this. He does not remember this. I am sure.
By now it must seem I hardly existed and what of it. The male toads
will trill that note all spring, as every spring, to bring the Beloved close
lest there be no sons of toads. And the night, I might not
remember as anything. I would walk up to his door and listen.
Sometimes in the distance a dog would bark. I would
stand there, my own breath loud, hearing when cupboards shut,
when water ran, their voices thick as blankets, silence.
I would fly back with my own angel now and slap myself.
But what do we do when someone doesn't want our love
and we must take it back, we must eat our own desire, and
slowly, slowly? At least I didn't knock. Not
after the first time. That year, I said goodbye to no one.
I took a bus and then a plane. There are those who cannot see in us
the shapely lantern or the few bright buds plum-red that brush against it.

But they show us it is there and then we ache. These May evenings,
I'm not all here. Not because I loved either man, really. But because
I learned then, and from loving since, who desire will make you betray,
what door you'll never knock on again. And then you do. Goddammit,
you do. You failing lantern. You bud. You will always
have to see for yourself. Tonight, the evening can't last
long enough. The moon-colored moths flutter up the ray
from the floodlight over the garage. Someone's left
their cap in my car and I am not going to return it. Screw the cap.
But all I speak of happened long ago, before the past
grew infinite. That's why tonight, even if a man was beautiful,
even if he played the guitar, and played a way that touched me,
I wouldn't go. I might gaze a while at his hands, watch
a shadow slip its girlish self inside his shirt. I might know
what it means to be the one and only one he's cruel to.
The truth is, the guitarist is old. He has lost a woman.
And all the good stories end when she is found,
when the round light of the lantern magnifies her form,
when the buds form their first kiss, when the breathlessness
is like a new body and the rain shines like honey on the leaves
outside the motel. But from there, the lovers have to go
somewhere. As we have had to go. It's why tonight
even if a man who was not a liar, a man who was burning,
a man with the smell of the sea on his neck, a man
who made my matter dance, leaned in and whispered

the places he'd take me sweet on his breath and his tongue, I
wouldn't listen, not even to the rain sweet-talking
the roof of the little blue motel where they drive up to the door
bearing the number of their room, the rain
ticking lightly on the car they sit kissing in after and before
she drives off alone until there are no cafés and no motels, no
doors or budding branches. But springs from now,
the toads whose bodies purr will fill the night. Someone we wanted once
will be a stranger or a ghost. Even if they say, Come back, be
young again, we will not listen. Desire tells a story
that is longer than we can bear.

MOTHERLAND

Mother painted blackbirds on the vaulted ceiling, a flock overhead against a light blue sky. The Romans used to paint their dining rooms, she told the girl. I'm starting a cornfield there on the north wall, she said pointing. As she pointed, she slowly turned until she was facing the west wall. The woods will start here. I'll have deer in it.

Each night the family had dinner, there was a little more countryside. The girl learned to eat with a deer staring at her from among the greenery.

It's like a picnic, Mother said, though the sky that showed above the trees was a darker blue, the color of morning glories, and Mother had painted a faint silver crescent moon. So the cornfield was day and the woods was evening and the east wall with the window was grazing land for the cows, black and white, as Mother had painted them, their heads lowered to the grass behind the electric fence.

Father said, If you keep this up, Mother, soon we'll have mosquitos. It'll rain too much.

I've always wanted to live here, said Mother spreading her arms out and turning around in a circle.

I've always wanted to live in San Francisco, but you don't see me painting the bedroom with little cable cars and Chinese restaurants, Father muttered.

Maybe we could keep one cow there by the buffet, Mother was saying. They each had a way of ignoring each other's part in the conversation the way married people do.

You can't eat the corn, Father said, so what's the point?

He could have his own door to go in and out. I'd spread a little straw on the floor . . .

Father heard her this time. You are not, he said, turning our dining room into a barn.

Mother replied, You turned our basement into a man-cave. I didn't object.

I wasn't bringing in livestock, he said.

Maybe a chicken. Or a rooster . . .

So the girl learned to eat dinner with a rooster pecking at her feet, with blackbirds painted on the ceiling, with rows of cornstalks in perfect perspective, with daylight on one wall and evening on the other, with one sad-eyed doe gazing out from the dark woods while Mother—Mother grew younger and more radiant, painted the window shade with lilac boughs and scattered seed on the floor for the rooster each morning and bought a little piglet who she suckled like an infant.

UNIFIED THEORY

The night is blue and staggered with stars.
Like you, I've tried to connect that one to
that one to that one to see the shapes that men
mapped ages ago, the Swan, the Archer pointing
his bow, but all I see are wayward rhomboids,
a leaning top hat, a celestial three-legged
insect the size of a country. Clouds
are easier, a lion, a bearded man, a lamb
bleeding into mist. We just want to recognize
where we are. Today was a good day or
a bad day. There are bills and laundry and
the thing your lover said and what you wanted.
If you stare a while the stars bounce in place,
nervous, and suddenly you wonder what
happened to all the ghosts in your second grade
class picture, wonder why you wonder . . . But what's
more important than the constellations? War?
Your broken dreams? The sink that swallowed
an earring? Tonight look up the light that left
Monoceros so many years ago. You get dizzy.
Is there life out there. Are there beings
like us. You too have scanned the tabloids
in the racks by the register, the blurry photos
of aliens with narrow heads, with no mouths,
with long arms and dangerous instruments

or telepathic powers, with pale skin, with scaly skin,
translucent skin or no skin at all, who've landed
always in remote woods, who've left carvings
on cave walls in Mongolia. But not one
says it. Not one headline proclaims we are
alone: THE ONLY CONSCIOUSNESS IN ALL
THE UNIVERSE AND IN ALL TIME. And tonight, what if,
what if we are? If we are a mere cosmic fluke. Or worse,
if we are so singly precious. I know you're just trying
to get by. Have stepped outside a second into your blue
body, to breathe, to trace the Little Dog constellation,
to watch the blinking halo of your TV from the wrong
side of your own window and behold
the living absence that your shape, alone, will fill.

ENCHANTED EGG #3

You see its interior moon, which is at first the only light. The walls are curved like the body of a bald airplane. Here, there is only waiting. The flowers are waiting to come up and die. The birds tick tick tick waiting to have their heart attacks. In the corner, the TV's blue aura flutters and licks the wall, while the girl sits and watches, waiting for the family to come on. Bang, bang, goes the TV, bang bang. Here, there is only one season. The potatoes stay buried till they are ghosts. A one-eyed car drives in the night around the snowy lake over and over in the same moment, so the distance never occurs. You see the moon in your brain like a shimmering gumdrop. Kiss, kiss, goes the TV. But Mother changes the channel and tells the girl, Wait till you're older. The ceiling is domed like the sky. Exactly what kind of space is this? What moon in what living room, what car revolving the pearl-faced lake—and the girl's broomstick horse laid next to the TV. It is like the little chaos one might find in a doll's head. Ha ha ha ha, the TV goes. From the kitchen Grandmother says, You don't appreciate your father. But Father is circling the frozen lake in his car, headlight poked in the dark. The trees are waiting to fall down, shore ice waiting to crack, a place becomes a minute. The moon absorbs your eye like a little pill. You'll always come back now. Baby, Baby, says the TV bouncing its reflection off the wallpaper rosettes and then begins to snow.

AUTUMN IN CALIFORNIA

—for Bruce

A deer was swimming in the surf
half mile out near Dana Point

people on the beach pointed
sea doe
nostrils stung with brine

carried over the blue green green
blue swell
toward some desire beyond

genus, until some longboarder
guided her back to shore, dying

wave gleaming like an eye,
the sunlight, the sand-mirror—

Where do you go
when you go?

Who called you?

Lucky I'm the age when I don't
expect answers.

The deer took off running
down the beach and bounded
back into the water

an almost perfect day
robin's egg sky
little wind

out there so little between
ecstasy and desperation,

What do you want
in the heave of a wave,
your hooves walking on water?

How is it to live your whole life
without a word—

Until you just start swimming.

3

POWER OUTAGE

—in memory, T. H.

Suddenly the world's blown out like a flame.
And there is only you

touching the house
while some *thing*
bangs into your shin and then

you stand still. The cat's fur
slides past coolly. At the window, shape is
deciding to be

a resemblance. We can't read.
We can't watch. We can't even admire
the red pumps we bought yesterday. It's black

as the past. It's black as
without. If you blink you don't know it.
O, it is ancient out.

And quiet. The cars only whisper. It was
over a year before I heard you died—
a queer feeling. It's a mistake to

depend on anything. We must
depend on everything, even the blackness,
even the void. What can I say, Tony,

that desire hasn't? That after an hour
it gets boring, sitting in the dark, waiting
to start your life over again, that

the later it gets the more the neighbor's pine
distinguishes itself in the breathiest
moonlight, March night, somewhere between

winter and spring and no more. Slowly,
the furniture assembles, the houses gather across
the street. In one window the beam of a flashlight

bounces up and down, right and left,
grows fitful. What are they
searching for? What have they lost?

Suddenly the light cut, the power gone,
the neighborhood is useless. Hard
not to let memory in then,

red pumps and all. Now the only light
left is the blinking light atop

the tower of the abandoned electric plant
a few miles down the coast,
a signal or a warning—to what

I don't know. It pulses like a big ruby
on and off on and off. Beyond it is the pitch
stretch of the sea. It will not

get an answer. Not tonight.
The house stays blind. Towns
disappear. Some

search for candles, some keep
pressing buttons. Some wait for sleep.
We are helpless for the moment.

For the moment we are night. And somewhere
a siren howls till the dogs sing terribly,
a portamento, the songs of their fleeting youth.

AMERICAN ALIEN

The truck ahead of me is American
with a bumper sticker that says NRA, and one
that recommends I *Cowgirl Up*
or Stay Home. Look at me
trying to look tough in my little car while
the silver silhouette of a naked woman
blinks at me from each mudflap, one
with wings and a halo, the other a tail
and horns. The sun flashes off their chrome
bodies as the flaps sway, naughty
and nice, strobing my eyes with nuclear
white light until I think maybe they're
bouncing signals to my brain and I'll
go out and buy boots, get a big dog, get
a Smith & Wesson and love my country.
My country

is the desert and it looks just like Iraq.
Here, we have a legislature
which decided we need a state gun,
after all we had a state bird and a state
flower. They also decided that guns
can go to college just like everyone
else. Meanwhile I watch the state birds
who've made a hole black as a socket

up in the saguaro they go in and out of.
This afternoon I'm headed home, still
a goddamn heathen pothead liberal
worried about animal extinction. Except
for the woodpecker who jackhammers
my roof early every morning. I know
my rights.

My rights are sweet sleep, good coffee
and Leave-Me-the-Fuck-Alone. I also
have a state bird and a state flower. I'm partial to
the local hummingbird, the blossoming
desert senna's fragrance and I'm voting for
a state disease. I lean toward manic-depression.
I lean toward those tiny gold blossoms
just to breathe the perfumed air above them before
they drop and pucker into dry brown kisses
and roam the earth. Then I think about
the driver of the truck, what kind of brain
she had, as if she were an alien, and did she
ride a horse named Misty did she even know
the history of anything before the millennium,
that nothing beats the thrill of putting the right
word in exactly the right place though we are
free in this country to put the wrong word

in the wrong place and run for office
and say you believe in freedom
when you really mean money.
My freedom,

her freedom, ours, theirs, it has always been
split between the angels of yes
and no, between *Honk if You Love Jesus* and
Send Every Juan Home, everyone on the open road
thinking they're going the right direction
as the cowgirl in her truck sticks her
pink fingernails out the window and adjusts
the side mirror before she pulls away. I'm thinking
about a state rock, igneous or
metamorphic. I'm thinking she voted
for the Sheriff who I hate and who, by the way,
has mandated a county underwear for inmates
which is dyed pink. It's one step toward
a state T-shirt to wear with our guns in bars
with cattle skulls hung on the wall alongside
the taxidermied specimen of a jackalope.
The shirt says *God Bless America*.
My shirt

says I'm suspect. My shirt says
It Is All a Political Hegemony Run by Arrogant
Short-sighted Reactionary Pimps for Corporations
Run by Weasels. And I'm watching the blue
metallic gleam of the tailgate as she turns
the corner and I get a whiff of
her music from the rolled down window,
a man with a twang singing *don't matter*
what went wrong, tonight I'm back where
I belong / tonight I'm—and the song drops
as she accelerates into the rest of her life
which I hope is happy,

happy as it can be for a half-angel half-bitch
driving her half-ton 4 x 4. May she
someday have a scandalous affair
with the deacon of her church or better yet
get caught naked in a motel with her lover
by her lover's wife, and bolt
right past her out the door and across
the parking lot wearing his T-shirt
bearing the image of Che Guevara
and ride home bare-ass in her truck
without hitting a single red light.

BLUE EURYDICE

She was blue as the mouth of a red rose,
as cognac set aflame in the spoon, as
the word *hinterland* with its blue ice
and gaunt blue rabbits, as little lights
along an airport runway, is what he,
Orpheus, thought that narrow second she
flashed before his eyes. He had wanted to
see she was still the Eurydice he knew
before she'd gone down to the underworld
and, of course, she was not. He thought at first
she had turned that color like certain birds
for mating season. It was shock—when form
comes undone easily. He could see near
the cave wall behind her the pile of arms . . .

She was blue as snow. Who had he loved, who?
Was Eurydice a ghost after all,
her beauty strange, estranging, tinged the hue
of the suffocated. Her face a fraud,
nostrils clotted with indigo, and eyes
like flame's iris. He was sick, and thralled
in all that twilight, when he saw her breasts
were the color of water, her sex, bruise—
he turned and heaved. Pain had been simple once.
We want back our lost ones, as if time moved
backward it would be the same. But it too
is loss, and loss our ravishment. He was
left her stain, Orpheus, and stepped from hell
a body midnight, the blue held by a hole.

BIRD OF PARADISE

The songs of the mariachi in the park
soar over the neighborhood. In the backyard
in the sea air I hear clearly the words
in Spanish which I don't speak
but I know the song is about a woman
and some man's heart like any song anywhere
though this one also seems to include
la niña linda and makes me suspect
the world of the mariachis is darker
than this summer night would have us
believing. On any given night along
these streets that lead to the beach
someone sets off firecrackers late
in the quiet. I believe they are members of
some secret club and the man down 4th street
is responsible for last Tuesday. The bang was
crisp and left the air ringing. Tonight
after the trumpets have spit and moaned nearly
two hours I am glad when the train
comes and drowns them in its animal cry.
Later it will come back through my sleep
mourning itself, hurtling north along the coast to
San Francisco. The mariachis are still here,
voices pouring through the open windows
of our rented cottage, making it harder to hear

the murder I'm watching on TV. I started to
watch a show where a mother talked about
the ghost in her child. She knew its name.
Who would believe the things people believe.
It's a while before I notice the music has left
only the breeze and the neighbor's wind chimes.
I never see her and he talks on the phone a lot.
On the other side, behind the high fence
the woman keeps calling the tall bird of paradise
a banana tree and it is scary how much
I want to launch myself over the fence and
correct the bitch. Which makes me suspect
my world is much darker than it appears.
Ay ay ay. The moon tonight is in its perigee,
whole and platinum, disfigured by its dark birthmark.
We stood on the front lawn for a good look.
I knew then summer was tucking itself into memory,
leaving us in the air. This was our greatness.
Time would go on without us and we
could not even hold on to each other.
Then a pop like a gunshot from the next street
loud enough to feel in your breastbone.
Then another. God
bless the assholes of the night
who keep us in the world which finally

grows still, the marine mist softening the houses,
erasing the hedge in front of the one that belongs
to the couple with a hundred screaming children
all of whom may have ghosts in them. The murder
I watched was about a woman and a man's
blackened heart. He dumped her body in the sea.
There is a song in this, *una canción*
en el mar. We want
to love forever like we want to answer
the long low wail of the train at night
with the hurt in our chest. Come back,
come back, little world. A teen-aged ghost boy rides
his skateboard sideways through the slow mist
into nothingness at the end of the block,
leaving us the séance of this street, its houses
hovering uncertainties, and the silvery
breath of the sea, and the sentience of the quiet
that comes at the end of music.

DRUNK AZURE

She held the nest which was wrong. But she was not yet old enough to leave a thing alone. One afternoon she had spotted it up in the rafters of the garage and had gotten up on the stepladder. Inside were three tiny eggs the color of sky, nestled, bald, alone as planets. It was their color that sank into her, that drunk azure, like a secret knowledge.

Each day she would climb up and check the nest. She never saw the mother. Maybe the mother had abandoned the eggs, the three of them blue as a lifting fever, smoother than the body. Up near the rafters it smelled like wood and dust.

But she was not yet old enough to keep a secret long. One afternoon she invited the neighbor girl to see the nest in the garage. At the top of the ladder she cupped her hands around the nest that was smaller than a teacup, lighter, and lifted it to show the girl clinging to the lower rungs. Then she placed it carefully back.

The neighbor girl had not appreciated their rarity nor would she fall under the spell of their dreamy blue.

The next time she entered the garage an egg had broken on the floor near the step, its yolk slipped out, deep yellow, the color she saw when she imagined the future. A bit of shell sat in gloss. She didn't see the nest, so she climbed the ladder and found it on its side on a shelf near the paint cans, one tiny egg half-crushed, the other still whole, blue as eyeshadow. Then she climbed down, shut the door and went out to play and spring passed. Enchantment was betrayed exactly by what it imagined. The color of the Greek sea in the sun, the color of rowboats. The broody turquoise beneath the wrist. The sequin glowing from the stereo in the dark living room.

If we could go back to our childhood we would be ravaged.

DANGER

The first time I saw the brain
someone was slicing it,
a gelid cauliflower, a wormy
loaf of bread. It was gross.
In eighth grade most things were.
Gross could be cool sometimes
like the car wrecks in an educational
film, actual footage. In this one
the brain was a drunk's
sliced open and compared to
some teatotaling old lady's which
had not been smoothed and shrunken
by Jack & Coke and launched
through the windshield when
the body it was cozy in and warm
drove head-on into a cop car. We
applauded. None of us were old enough
to drive or buy a beer but we
were warned. Never let it be said
we weren't. But it meant nothing then
beyond a half hour in the dark during the day,
time we could make the shadows
of obscene gestures play across the screen,
send messages across the room and
draw pictures of the teacher with horns

and a fat ass and warts. I've forgotten her,
and most of them, but the gray runnels
of the human brain cut open remain all too
fresh, naked their uselessness, more
lunar than human, because it was,
for Chrissake, an actual brain from inside
of all of us, this blanched withered sliceable
meatloaf, which *was* actually us. That
was gross. And subtly terrifying. If we
were only matter we were in danger.
And it was hard enough being matter at 13
not a pickled cerebellum but a matter changing
shape too quickly. Think
about that. It wasn't the lesson
I was supposed to take away. I was supposed to
stay away from alcohol and drugs. Sorry.
Life is short. It falls too
easily from the knife, that wedge of bloated sotted
lace that thought it held so much.

THE DARK AGES

My brother taught me
how to lie on your back under a tree
during a tornado warning
in Wichita Falls, Texas, and look up
the big branches rowing in the wind
the dim leaves bending back
until you were dizzy and the sky
turned purple. Everything
smelled like electricity. That summer
he also taught me to lie in the living room
and listen through special Quadrophonic
headphones to Joe Cocker and
eat a head of lettuce when I was stoned.
These were valuable lessons. No matter
where the drinking took him
later. Over us flashed crippled
forks of lightning while the fleeing
dust and grit bit our skin. We
kept our backs against the earth
like a door. The tree stood alone,
dark, wildly gesturing, *here, here.*
I felt I must go. But then
I could smell every molecule
rising from the backyard, I
could smell the basement

of the first house I lived in, and the leaves
flipped showing their silver nap
as they held on. There was a moment
I thought we might stay until
our bodies were caught up
and tumbled like two straws
in galloping infinity. It was the dark
ages of summer and I felt
everything true and golden
was written in a book I could not read.
I'd come back nights from
my shit job, crack open a new
pack of menthols from the fridge
while my brother rolled a joint
and told some story from before
I was born. We'd smoke
and lie back in the music and
Cocker's voice like sexed-up
gravel made us clean as clouds
on a postcard. What came later
wasn't born yet. You have to take
your grace where you find it.

X

Sometimes I come out of my life
with missing you

then I'm good for nothing.
Today is burning; it's late September.

At night the Big Dipper almost touches the ground.
Sometimes with remembering, I pour

out of my life, formless again. Look at the stars.
Mostly I get along—I write.

Everyone says if it doesn't cool off soon
they're going to kill someone.

Your smile, your smile, your voice, your hands, your teeth—

Sometimes with disbelief
I stare at my life.

Cruelty's no more than mathematics.
X ≠ comfort.

I've gone as far as to wish there is a God.
And then to take issue with him.

You were brave to live, I say to absence,
I say to us, maybe

to everyone. Sometimes I just watch
one star at a time. The air is warm

as fur. Coyotes shriek just over there—
break out in death laughter. I

find it comforting. I really do.
I like the company

of something we will never understand.
It means there's more

than us. And good for it—may it prosper.
I am hurt with you.

I am unbearably sane. I have nothing
to believe. I'd take Sunday breakfasts

the booth orange vinyl and right by the window,
as always, in a coffee shop

as gone as the child in it. It's what I'm good for—
Imagine, then

mourn the imagined: You
the blue light at the end of the mind,

staying there, small blue x,
glowing above the dark road

where grief becomes love again.

FOR MIGUEL IN VENICE

The prism-necked pigeons follow you everywhere.
They sit puffed up like rainclouds beneath your table, one
on the seat of the chair across. Let him eye you. Whoever
you were somewhere else is a ghost. You
have returned to the old world, shadows stretched
in the late light, the sinking
palaces, the windows filled with water, the old world
at ease with death. Melon rinds bob carelessly
floating under the bridge, later, where you stop
to watch the moon scattered on the dark canal.
Only where the light falls can you see the water thinking.
I want to tell you a few nights ago
the cat brought me a dark gift in her mouth
and laid it down on the floor, still moving. It was
small as a man's thumb, a newborn rat with
closed eyes and a pink belly. When I nudged it
with a piece of cardboard, it flexed its toes,
lifted its arms. I shivered. I did not want to
touch him. The cat wanted to bat him around
for a while. We both had our primitive reasons.
I tell you just to let you know things
back here are sad and extraordinary. You
make out with the hairdresser, walk home
in the city's blackness and gloss, city like the wet dream
of Edgar Poe were he Italian. The hairdresser

follows you everywhere. When you turn around
he disappears. You can smell the water.
Along the edge the black-prowed gondolas tied up
jostle like horses. Everyone is asking
why you've stayed so long and when
you're coming back. But I say stay
if you want to. Die there. Who doesn't wish
dreams were money. Take the winged lions
and fly them off the golden dome of San Marco
and fuck anyone who says it can't be done.
Plenty can be done in beauty that can't be
in the world. Here the dry winter
has made me want to sleep, to burrow like the rabbits
under the cholla. I want to lie in bed and inhale
the clean sheets of my childhood. I want to rest
and hold on. But I was disturbed that night
by a life I didn't want. I bent down, slid the cardboard
under, stood up with the thing squirming on it, and
began to carry it somewhere—not outside
in the cold—somewhere. I laid him by the wall
next to the shelves in the garage. He lay on his side,
curled. We had two rat traps near the door.
They'd eaten papers in a storage box, left their scat.
Yet I looked down at that tiny thing
and got it in my head I needed to keep him warm

at least and came back with an old knitted cap
which he grasped at as I rolled him onto it
and folded it over him like an orange wool cave.
I knew he was going to die. You say
you've seen two rats in Venice, one running
by you the night you fell in love with the opera house.
You say everything was dripping with jewels—
Some afternoons you take the boat to the cemetery,
your namesake, San Michele. You like the view from there
looking back at the city, the single spruce charcoal
and blue smudge against the winter sky. We cannot
look at the world enough. Things here
are ridiculous and fragile. I mean Goddammit.
I couldn't sleep. How bewildering it must be
for a body, suddenly pushed into the wombless air,
blind, hairless, born dying for touch.
And hungry. So believe I went back into the garage
with a Q-tip dipped in milk and tried to swab
the baby rat's mouth which never opened. His body
stretched out so I saw his pink underside, his
delicate hands and feet which curled around
the stick and tried to hold it. This plague.
This filthmonger. This breath. Tell me
if I was stupid or just crazy and what I should have done.
Tell me how the hairdresser had some drawings

by Michaux and knew the French ambassador
who served you tea in his study wearing velvet slippers.
Life is wretched. You admit you'll come back
for your medicine, you miss your dog.
I'm never going anywhere again. I mean it.
I couldn't sleep. I couldn't go back in the garage.
I couldn't be the crazy woman growing old raising
her rat-child. It was cold out, but I stood there
for some time, the full moon a fairy gold
floating in the blackness which contained
all largeness, all intimacies, and smelled sweet
bittersweet like the creosote. We learn
to love beauty most for its disregard.

GOOD MYSTERY

Mother pointed to the distance. A great
wave of blackbirds was moving toward us
in the blue sea up there. When they were right
over us, she said, I would see the red
beneath their wings. Spread above the field they flew
like one mind, a hundred small darknesses
quivering in it. I waited, tilted
my head back. It was a shock that scarlet
flashing out from the utter black, the birds
flickering not only with red but with
bright yellow, the secret my mother had
not told me. The yellow was the yellow
of bees. The red was the red of the poppies
old men wore on Memorial Day. Who
would want an afterlife after this
body of heaven, these birds beautiful
as wounds, even if it was long ago,
long enough that it might have been a dream,
and the light left only its delicate
smell on my forehead. The dizziness of
looking up was like seeing backward
till leaving was coming, till birds were
flowers that bloomed over and over,
the old heart, the young heart, the same
good mystery. As children our great joy

is to study the things of this world which
seems infinite. And when we are old we
take up this joy again, watching the field
stir, insects swoon in the golden dander,
charting the morphologies of cloud beasts,
this time because it is finite as if
we pressed the earth to our breast. What we know
of life we know of death, that black scorch with
a flame beneath each wing. I know blackbirds
waved their cape over us on their way to
the distance, showing us their hearts, and the place
where my mother and I were standing became
the past, singular, eternal, and of
no earthly use.

ROOMS BY THE BEACH

Sometimes when I look up at the stars I forget everything I know.
The world is neither happy nor unhappy. Early summer,
night as warm as skin, and on the mountain slope one house
is lit up for a party. The huff of a car door, the trebles of laughter,
drift down to the private darkness, the desert all scratch and shadow.
The guests must be beautiful and rich. Above them hang
the stars of the Great Bear glittering eagerly—
I'd come outside to look at the sky during a party once,
people stood with their cocktails around the pool
with its underwater light opening its large blue eye. A man and I
made small talk, what he did, what I did, who we knew.
When he heard I knew Marie he told me he'd been wanting
to meet her but she was, he said, so beautiful and around
beautiful women he got tongue-tied. And then
he asked if I would introduce him. I looked at him
hard. Tonight, looking at the windows of the house up there,
each the same gold that bleeds off into the black
of all form, I try to think when had something, or someone,
beautiful rendered me speechless, heart in my throat . . .
though I have been silent enough now in the middle of
some magnificent dream: The trill of desert toads
waiting for water in the arroyo, the tiny gecko crawling
the cement stoop, the delicate tick of dry seedpods
falling from the old palo verde. Somewhere not to
have to be. The haze of a few monsoon clouds slides

past the low half-moon. But back at the party Marie
was chatting with a couple in the corner. I hadn't known
that she was beautiful, her short brown hair, wide face,
small flat lips, her figure full and beginning to go to fat.
She did have pretty eyes, dark as coffee, and a nice smile.
I wasn't being bitchy. And the man I had been talking with
was just another lawyer writing a novel. Though there was a waiter
at the Cuban restaurant who was more gorgeous than any man
had the right to be, had dark eyes a woman could fall into, a form
so fine she dreamed herself against him, and forgave
the wilted salad or the tardy glass of wine, and still I
could articulate the fact the fish was underdone and when he tried
to tell me it was cooked correctly, leaning over and smiling and, yes,
beautiful, ladies, wild horse beautiful—I smiled back and said
the flesh should not be translucent, showed him with my fork.
His hair was chestnut in the light. And, for half a second,
the cherry wood gleaming in a room of my childhood. Then I was back
watching him disappear with the fish into the steamy kitchen like
a mirage. Like the white half-moon behind the boulders
balanced on the southern ridge this evening, the ghosts
of headlights from the mountain road swinging out to
the middle of nothing. All we are is light. We are traveling always,
each a radiating body losing itself in its beholding and, in its long desire,
already a past. It's in our DNA, the lonesome glitter of our cells
emitting photons. We are never in one place. Tonight, I'm at the party,

tonight I'm standing in the dark behind my house where the desert
starts to rise to the mountain, the air humid, scented with resin.
No rain in five months. Two mule deer stood not far from here
earlier, down among the houses, looking for water, a young buck
whose antlers were beginning to bud, another, older, who stared
at me a long time. I was perfectly still. It seemed to me
I could feel his gaze and my own strangeness—while the young one
chewed leaves from the mesquite. I could feel his gaze
and my changing because of it and my loneliness because of it.
And my dying. And my beauty. Tonight, I'm in the dimness of
the parking lot behind the restaurant, the waiter smoking
with his back leaned against the dumpster half in shadow.
His face looked more brutal, then handsome, but brutal,
like he could love you and still slit your throat. Then
he smiled. I don't remember how we got to talking—he
was from Modesto, came here after a woman but, he said,
it didn't work out. He still pulled her picture from his wallet
and held it up under the light so I could see. There was the face
of a woman I'd never met and never would, her eyes light blue
like rooms by the beach. Some things you remember too clearly
and you have no idea why they come to you on a June night
under the stars watching the house on the slope glow
like a small hope in the black air. From there they must see
the city spilled out, twinkling, below. From here I can
look back on my own window holding the chair and the desk

as I left them. I am always imagining the world where I am
dead. Telling myself this is how it will look. It will look
like her eyes, the waiter's woman, an empty bed, a cotton shirt
draped on a chair. Everything a reflection. Who knows
if what the eye sees is what the mind sees much less
the heart, if you call it that, that place in us
that aches when we love. Everywhere we look in the night sky
a world is burning, a world of then, a world of now, a world
of never and ever. A world of Marie—turning in her violet dress
near the table with the coffee urn, silver earring sending
a spark. Like I said, that night when he asked me to approach her
I looked at him hard, pretty sure I was going to tell him
to go fuck himself. He was a man a little heavy, going bald,
a sloped and shining forehead, a thick nose, a man
whom probably no beautiful woman would ever talk to,
a man so fearful of beauty it struck him dumb. Then
I took him gently by the arm, led him across the patio,
past the potted palms, past the cluster of women with wine,
past the Mexican mask hung near the sliding glass door,
to where she was standing and introduced him. She smiled
as he cleared his throat, swallowed a couple times and stammered
it was nice to meet her. He didn't notice when I let go of his arm
and slipped away. Once, as I was leaving, I looked back
and glimpsed him through the happy windows of that house
which seemed to hold a world far away and going beautifully without me

as it must, tonight, up there on the slope and further out where
so many stars are I lose my head. I lose. Everyone. Even the waiter
who was still bent over her eyes when I said good night, as if,
if he looked long enough, she'd appear. Lately, everywhere I go
someone is wounded or about to be, everywhere someone
has been left behind or left someone or loved someone who never came.
It is easy to believe the stars know more than we do,
seeing us always in their past. The animals have gone back
to the mountain. The house on the mountain has gone dark.
Still, we see as we see in dreams, hunched in our own light
that just this afternoon two deer passed through. Look long.
The night is warm, golden Arcturus is pulsing and the faint
smell of monsoon two days off is almost sweet. Someone
has left us here and slipped away. The darkness is rich tonight,
its guests are beautiful. How can we not speak?

ACKNOWLEDGMENTS

Thank you to the editors of the following publications where these poems appeared:

Catamaran: "Petaloudes," "Enchanted Egg #2"; *Connotation Press*: "The Door"; *Field*: "My Neighbor's Body"; *Fifth Wednesday*: "Bees on Cocaine"; *Hayden's Ferry Review*: "Birds of Darkness Inhabit the Night, Stars on Their Foreheads"; *Hamilton Stone Review*: "My Rain"; *Lake Effect*: "Good Mystery"; *The Laurel Review*: "X," "My Science"; *Plume*: "An Occupation," "Bird of Paradise," "Henry's Song," "Hot Pink," "The Dark Ages," "Unified Theory," "Enchanted Egg #1," "Enchanted Egg #3"; *Plume Anthology 3*: "Music at an Exhumation"; *Plume Anthology 4*: "For Miguel in Venice"; *Plume Anthology 5*: "American Alien"; *Plume Anthology 10*: "Autumn in California"; *Spillway*: "Blue Euridyce," "Rooms by the Beach"; *Tuesday: An Art Project*: "Danger."

Some of the poems have also appeared in *The Best American Poetry 2013* and *The Pushcart Prize Anthology 2014*.

Special thanks to Miguel Murphy for his invaluable help with the manuscript.